Date: 1/21/22

BR 598.53 NIL
Nilsen, Genevieve,
Emu chicks /

TOOLS FOR CAREGIVERS

- **F&P LEVEL:** D
- **WORD COUNT:** 34
- **CURRICULUM CONNECTIONS:** animals, habitats

Skills to Teach

- **HIGH-FREQUENCY WORDS:** are, have, on, their, they, this
- **CONTENT WORDS:** beaks, chicks, dad, eat, eggs, emu, green, grow, hatch, lose, run, sits, small, stripes, up, use
- **PUNCTUATION:** exclamation points, periods
- **WORD STUDY:** /k/, spelled *ck* (*chicks*); long /e/, spelled *ea* (*beaks*, *eat*); long /e/, spelled *ee* (*green*); /oo/, spelled *u* (*emu*); long /o/, spelled *ow* (*grow*)
- **TEXT TYPE:** factual description

Before Reading Activities

- Read the title and give a simple statement of the main idea.
- Have students "walk" through the book and talk about what they see in the pictures.
- Introduce new vocabulary by having students predict the first letter and locate the word in the text.
- Discuss any unfamiliar concepts that are in the text.

After Reading Activities

Emu chicks are born with stripes. As they grow up, their stripes fade. Their feathers turn tan and brown like their dad's. Can readers name any other animals that have patterns on their feathers or skin? Do these patterns change at any time? What other changes do readers notice between the emu chicks and the emu dad in the book?

Tadpole Books are published by Jump!, 5357 Penn Avenue South, Minneapolis, MN 55419, www.jumplibrary.com

Copyright ©2022 Jump. International copyright reserved in all countries. No part of this book may be reproduced in any form without written permission from the publisher.

Editor: Jenna Gleisner **Designer:** Molly Ballanger

Photo Credits: CraigRJD/iStock, cover, 2tl, 2tr, 2br, 8–9, 10–11, 12–13; K.A.Willis/Shutterstock, 1; Bill Bachman/Alamy, 2ml, 3; Marina Kryuchina/Shutterstock, 2mr, 4–5; Fred Bavendam/SuperStock, 2bl, 6–7; Ken Griffiths/Shutterstock, 14–15; JensenChua/iStock, 16.

Library of Congress Cataloging-in-Publication Data
Names: Nilsen, Genevieve, author.
Title: Emu chicks / by Genevieve Nilsen.
Description: Minneapolis: Jump!, Inc., 2022. | Series: Outback babies | Includes index. | Audience: Ages 3–6
Identifiers: LCCN 2020047884 (print) | LCCN 2020047885 (ebook) | ISBN 9781645279433 (hardcover)
ISBN 9781645279440 (paperback) | ISBN 9781645279457 (ebook)
Subjects: LCSH: Emus—Infancy—Juvenile literature.
Classification: LCC QL696.C34 N55 2022 (print) | LCC QL696.C34 (ebook) | DDC 598.5/241392—dc23
LC record available at https://lccn.loc.gov/2020047884
LC ebook record available at https://lccn.loc.gov/2020047885

EMU CHICKS

by Genevieve Nilsen

TABLE OF CONTENTS

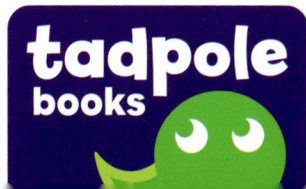

tadpole
books

WORDS TO KNOW

beaks

chicks

dad

eggs

hatch

stripes

EMU CHICKS

emu ▶

This emu dad
sits on eggs.

3

egg

They are green!

5

Chicks hatch.

chick

They are small.

stripe

They have stripes.

They run!

They eat.

beak

They use their beaks.

They grow up!

They lose their stripes.

15

LET'S REVIEW!

How many emu chicks do you see with Dad?

INDEX